I0486591

The Wedding Picture

A Wedding Photographer's Guide
To Getting Great Wedding Pictures

Photos & text by Andrea Sperling

To Grace

Copyright © 2007 by Andrea Sperling
ISBN: 978-1-4303-2809-4
All rights reserved including the right of reproduction in
whole or in part in any form whatsoever.

Photos & text © Andrea Sperling

INTRODUCTION

Over the past 10 years, I've photographed hundreds of weddings. Big weddings, small weddings, celebrity weddings, and weddings in vineyards, barns and boats.

I've shot weddings where the bride doesn't talk to her family and weddings where the bride and groom have spent most of the wedding sitting in a corner kissing, oblivious to everyone, including the photographer!

There have been weddings I've shot that have taken two years to plan where I was involved during the entire process, and then there was the engagement party where the couple announced during the toasts that they were turning it into a wedding. I guess they wanted to surprise everyone, including the photographer.

In addition to clicking the shutter, I've lovingly acted as therapist, event planner, organizer, stylist, diplomat and best friend to the bride and groom and their guests.

I've even contributed photos to several wedding books, including *Emily Post's Wedding Book*, *A Wedding For All Seasons* and Portal Publication's *Wedding Planner*.

So I guess you can say that I know a lot about weddings and wedding photography. I've also made it a point to ask everyone whose wedding I *haven't* shot to tell me about his or her wedding pictures. I guess I did this partly to size up the competition, and partly to see if there was anything brilliant they had done that I might have done myself.

And now I've moved on from shooting weddings to the world of the web. Shooting weddings have been a great experience – I got to be a part of one of the most intimate, special days of people's lives, I got to see people at their best and I got to eat great wedding cake, too! No wonder I've befriended so many of the couples I've worked with and have had the pleasure to photograph many of their children, too, over the years.

On the other side, shooting lots of weddings takes its toll. It's kind of scary to know that you only have one chance to get it right. A still life photographer can rearrange the fruit arrangement he is photographing a million times until he gets it right. You can't imagine a wedding photographer asking the bride and groom to repeat their vows again in front of 200 people in the middle of a church ceremony because the flash didn't go off! We just can't make a mistake and that's VERY nerve racking.

It's also a very long day for us. We get home in the wee hours of the morning. And for those of us with kids, it can be kind of difficult because then we get the 6 a.m. "MOMMY!" wake-up call. So we're always sleep deprived. And then there's the physical wear and tear on our bodies - the bad backs from carrying bags of equipment, the carpal tunnel syndrome and the eyes going bad.

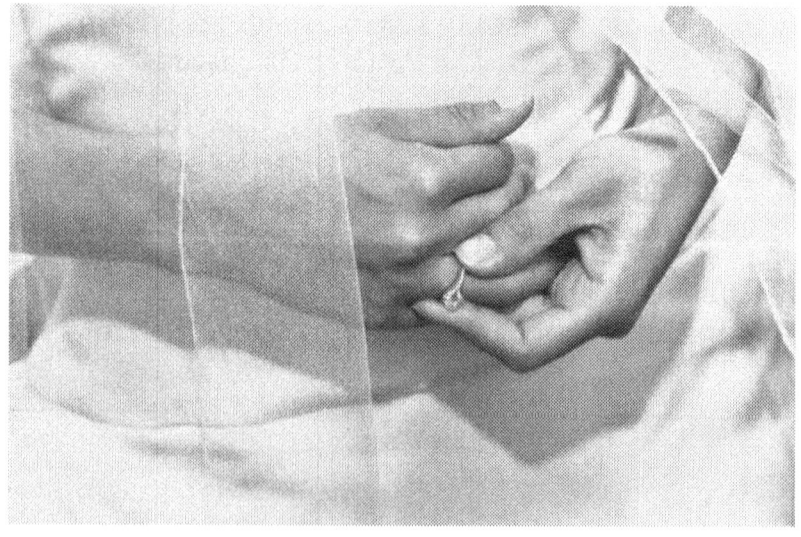

All in all, I'm glad I shot weddings for so many years. I learned to think fast on my feet and I provided people with a useful service. I especially was grateful when I would run into someone whose wedding I shot years later and they would say something like "That photo you took of my grandfather at my wedding is the last picture of him looking happy before he got sick and passed away so I just want to thank you for capturing him so well."

The most important thing I learned about shooting weddings is that things happen. It can rain on your outdoor wedding. The bride's dress can get a stain on it BEFORE she's even walked down the aisle. The minister can be 45 minutes late. Or the irresistibly cute little flower girl can have a temper tantrum in the middle of the ceremony. I've learned that the people who just take the Zen approach – take a deep breath, relax and handle it with grace are the ones who have the best time at their weddings. And they get the best pictures, too.

I've learned this, too: the most important thing about getting good wedding pictures is communication and collaboration. In a sense, you're almost marrying the photographer for the day, too.

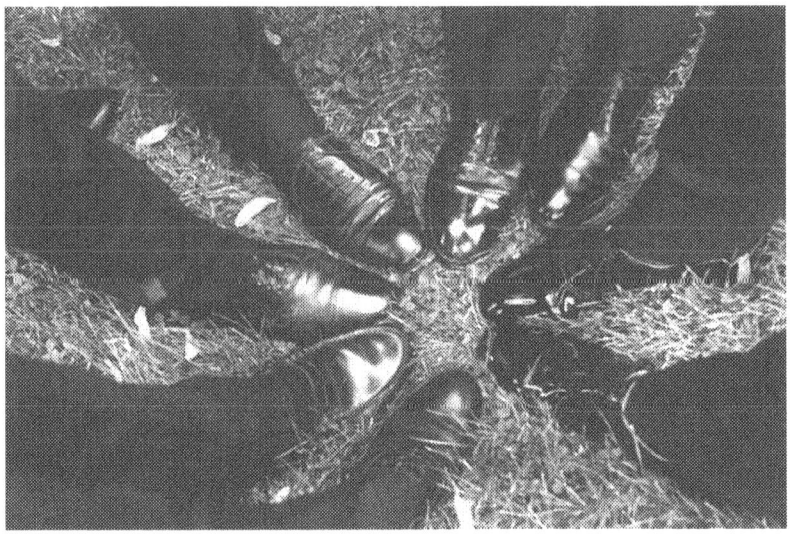

TYPES OF WEDDING PHOTOGRAPHERS

There are basically two kinds of wedding photographers- studio photographers and photojournalists or "art" photographers. The most important thing is that you like their style. Whether they shoot digitally or with film is not as important. (More on this later.)

STUDIO PHOTOGRAPHERS

When you contact a big wedding studio you'll notice that they generally have a group of photographers you can choose from at different price ranges. Some have different styles. Traditionally, they shoot a limited number of images – the classic wedding shots and the group shots.

Before digital, studio photographers used to mostly shoot with medium format cameras like a Hasselblad. These camera were great because the images would have less grain and as a result, the pictures are very crisp and can retain a lot of detail. The down-side is that medium format is a lot slower and since you'd only get 12 shots to a roll, you had to change film often. The photographer can't be so spontaneous, so you get less creativity and more posed pictures.

Also, with this sort of approach, you're generally tied to a package that the studio has – you have a choice of one kind of album and the package comes with approximately 50 8 x 10's or some specific combination. It's great if you're the kind of person who needs to know exactly what you're getting and wants a traditional album and layout.

When working with a big studio sometimes you don't get to meet the photographer ahead of time. I encourage you to only work with a studio where you can meet with the photographer ahead of time. And you must see that person's portfolio and website, if they have one. You need to be able to communicate with the photographer to let them know *who's* important and *what's* important to you. While all weddings are the same in some ways, they are also different in many other ways and a photographer shouldn't just only shoot the "formula" shots.

PHOTOJOURNALISTS

For lack of a better word, photojournalists like to tell a story in their pictures. They use smaller format 35 mm cameras that allow them to shoot faster. This allows them to "capture the moment." They'll also shoot a lot more film or digital images than the studio photographer.

Their packages vary and their prices vary a lot, too. Personally, I took pictures in the "photojournalist" style. I liked the spontaneity of it. I liked giving my clients a lot of choices – not just formally posed images but a range of images that offered a sense of the people, the location, and the mood of the day. I also loved shooting all the details –from the flowers to all the other personal touches that were so meticulously arranged for the occasion.

I also offered my clients a range of album choices and sizes. My feeling was that everyone had his or her own individual taste and the client should get a variety of choices. I always went for the middle route- I called it "classic with a twist."

In the best of all worlds, you want to make sure you have someone who can take the group shots and do them well and also capture all the great moments in an interesting, artful way. Some photojournalists shy away from any portraiture or group shots so if you want that, make sure they have some images to show you.

Someone once said to me "I want my pictures to look like Richard Avedon shot me and Henri Cartier Bresson shot the rest of the pictures." For those of you who don't know who these great photographers were – the sentiment is that the bride wanted to make sure she looked beautiful in all the shots (like the great fashion photographer Richard Avedon) and that the pictures captured the "decisive moment" as the seminal photojournalist Henri Cartier Bresson said. Who could blame her?

SECOND SHOOTERS AND ASSISTANTS

In my opinion, a photographer -whether a photojournalist who likes to roam the room or a studio photographer- needs to bring an assistant. They should incorporate the assistant's fee into their fee. The assistant helps the photographer schlep their gear and keep track of it but also is invaluable of helping with troubleshooting if the photographer should be having any technical problems. (I always kept mine on flash patrol to make sure the flash was always going off).

A good assistant helps expedite the group shots by organizing and arranging everyone so the photographer can keep shooting.

A great assistant can help out a little with shooting when you can't be two places at once- if for example, during the ceremony, there's a balcony to get an overview of the service, the assistant can get that shot while the main photographer stays upfront.

A second shooter is necessary under a few conditions. If you're having a large wedding, it's great to have another person. My cut-off point was if there were over 150 people, it would be helpful to have another photographer. If your wedding is at a sprawling facility, then it would also be helpful to have cameras in various locations. Also, if you have a large wedding and want table shots, then the second shooter could shoot the tables while the main photographer works the room so they don't miss any of the good stuff!

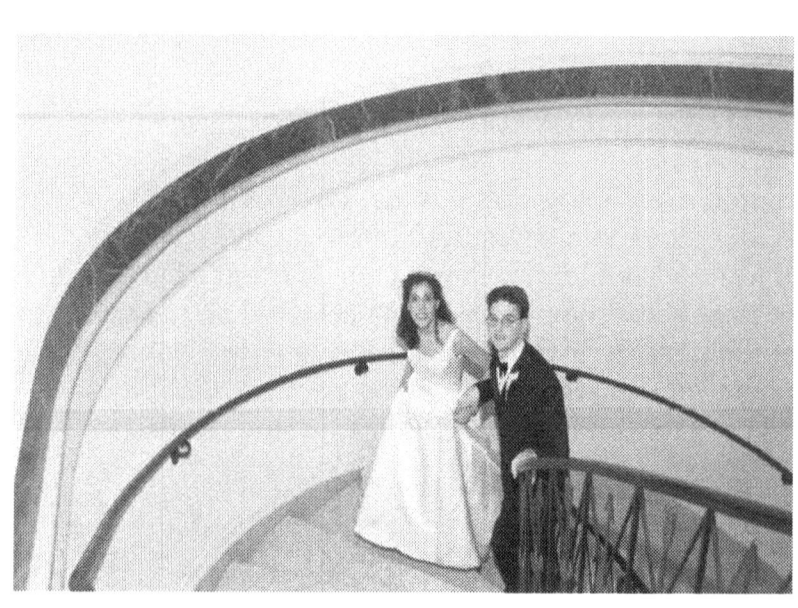

SHOOTING DIGITALLY VS SHOOTING WITH FILM

Most studios and photojournalists can shoot your wedding digitally now. As the technology improves, digital wedding photography gets better and better. You can have your images uploaded to a website and if you want, you can have digitally scanned photos in your albums.

Some photographers will only shoot digitally- they prefer the workflow and it allows them to shoot more and see what they're doing as they work so they can catch any mistakes. They will either upload the images onto a website for you to see and then you can order prints, or they will have proofs and enlargements made from the digital files.

Other photographers still use film as their preference because they like the way the pictures reproduce, especially enlarged black and white images. They will shoot the wedding using film and then give you proof prints and enlargements. Some photographers will offer to have the negatives scanned so they can be uploaded to a website and then give you proofs, too. This is usually a bit more expensive but gives you alittle of both worlds. All approaches have their advantages and disadvantages for both the photographer and the client. Find the approach that is suitable for your needs and budget.

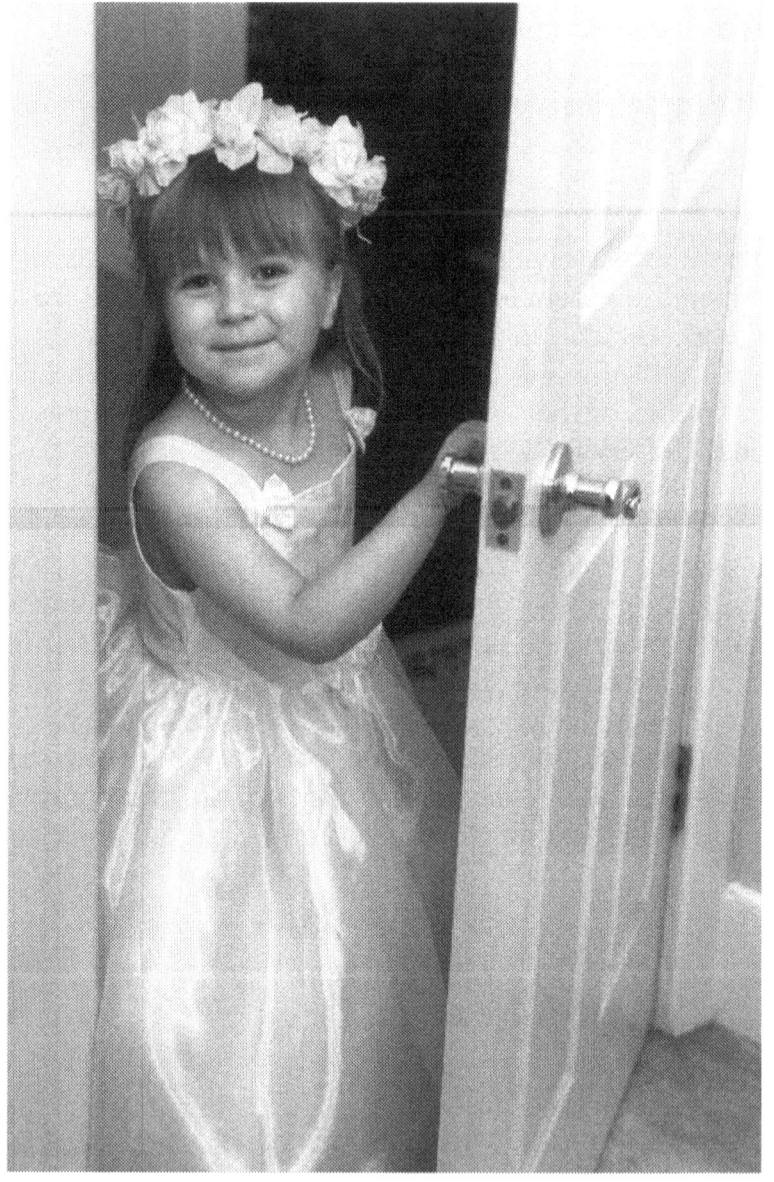

CONTRACTS AND PACKAGES

The most important thing I can tell you in this book is to make sure you have a written contract - even if you have a friend or relative shoot the wedding.

Everyone has a different price range and different packages. Make sure you really understand what's included in the package-from hours and overtime, to proofs, enlargements and websites. What happens if the photographer gets sick at the last minute and can't show up? Will the photographer be responsible for getting a suitable replacement? What if the reception is running later than you booked the photographer for - is overtime included in the contract or is there an extra fee? Can you buy or keep the negatives or have a CD later with the images to keep?

WEB PACKAGES VS. PROOFS

As mentioned earlier, some packages include just the shoot and the proofs, and final albums with enlargements are separate. Other packages include the shoot, proofs and an album with enlargements. Still others offer the shoot and everything uploaded onto a website or they'll give you the images on a CD. If you're on a tight budget, this is generally a less expensive approach because it involves less work and expense from the photographer's end. From there, you would purchase everything off the web.

So think about what you ultimately want. Some people want to have their pictures posted on the web if there are a lot of out-of-towners. If your mother lives on the east coast and your mother-in-law lives on the west coast, having the pictures on the web is a great way for everyone to see the pictures. And if you don't have the resources or desire to pay for reprints for your family and friends, this is a good way for them to purchase enlargements or reprints independently.

On the other hand, if you're like me, you still want to physically leaf through hundreds of pictures so getting proofs that you can show everyone is helpful. Another reason having proofs is good is that the website won't be up forever so it's good to have hard copy of everything, too. (Not to mention the fact that some people, especially older people, aren't web savvy.) And if you go for an option where you just get a CD or DVD with all the images, remember that these forms of media will be obsolete one day and then you'll have to convert them to something else. So make sure you have prints, too.

Lastly, if a photographer offers you a web package only and then you decide later that you also want 4 x 6 prints of all the images, you're going to end up spending a lot of extra money that you hadn't thought of before. If the photographer can make the prints upfront of everything, they will generally cost less than if you purchase them off the web one at a time. So really think about what you'll really want not just for the short term but the long term. Do the math. Ask questions.

KEEPING NEGATIVES AND CD'S

And what about the negatives? If the photographer is shooting film, can you keep the negatives after the wedding? Or do you have to purchase them? Some photographs will never let you purchase the negatives or obtain a CD with the images on them. Other photographers will let you purchase the negatives or scans after you've made your enlargements and album. It's a way for the studio to have quality control and to have another source of income. And personally, photographers put a lot of time into giving their customers quality work so I think it's always a better idea to have the photographer make the enlargements. I would always at least have the photographer make your final album with the enlargements and the initial reprints for your families.

If the photographer shoots everything digitally, can you purchase a CD with all the pictures or can you purchase a CD with all the images at some point after you've made enlargements? The idea is that if the photographer should move and you have no way of getting in contact with them in 10 years and you want some reprints, how can you make sure you can do this? And will the CD be low resolution jpgs or higher resolution tif files? When you're planning the wedding, this is too far in the future, so quite often people don't think about this and are upset about this later.

So ask questions! To me, the worst thing a photographer (or any business professional) can do is to surprise a client about financial matters. Every single expense that can be incurred should be listed in the contract and you should read it carefully and ask questions. You don't want to work with people who have hidden costs that are not in their contracts.

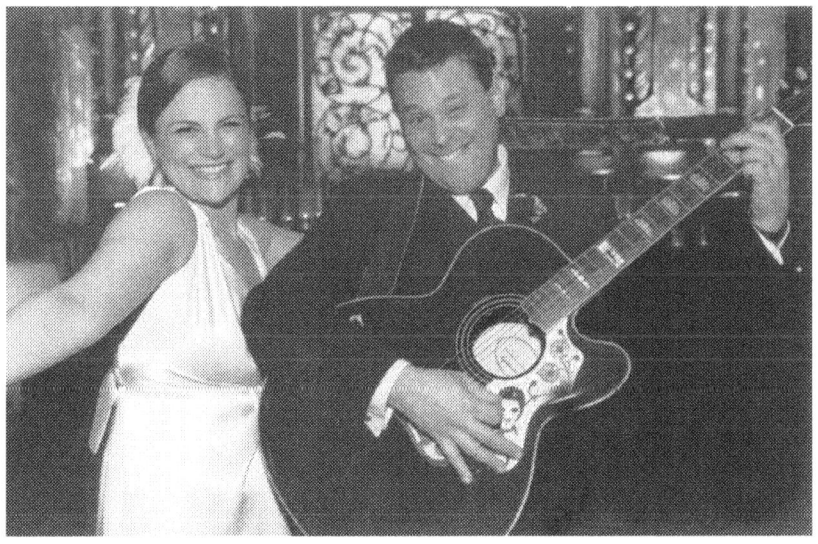

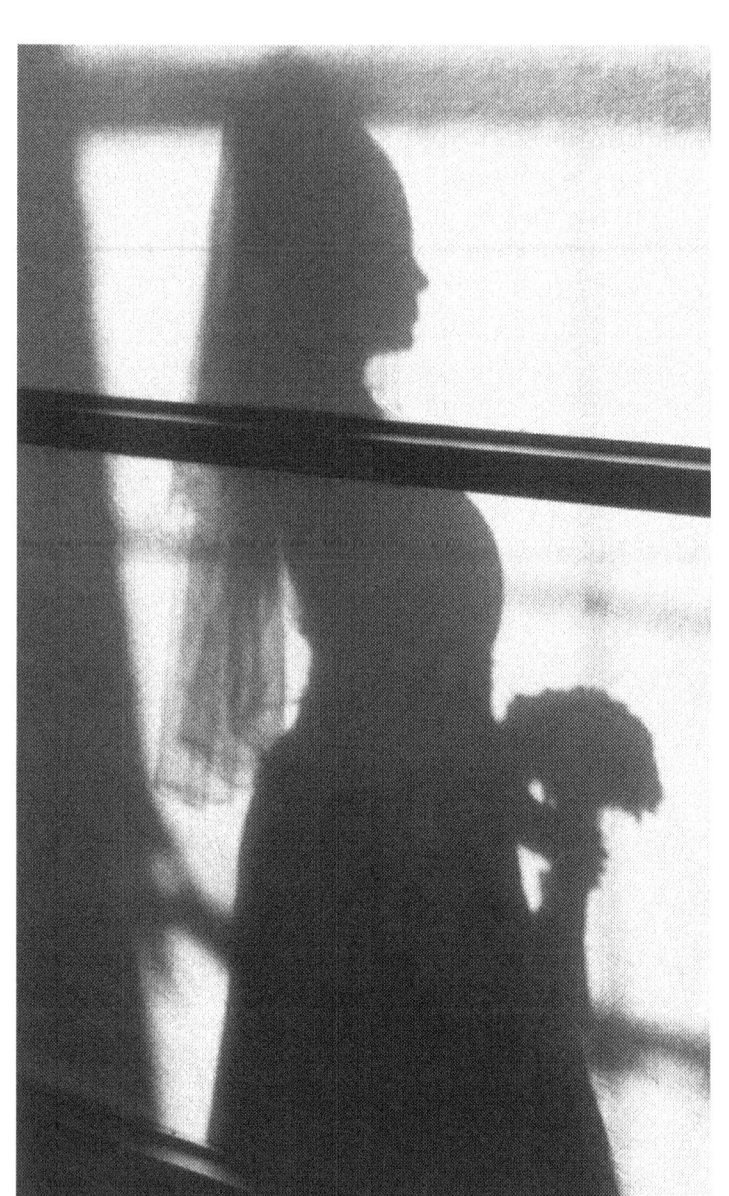

HOW TO FIND A PHOTOGRAPHER

Referrals: Ask some of your friends about the photographer they used for their wedding. Look at their photographs (hopefully they have a website, too) and if you like them, contact that photographer. If they tell you they are booked, ask them if they can recommend anyone else. Most photographers know a lot of other great photographers that they've worked with before, trained or just admire.

Websites: Do a web search. Use the keywords "wedding" "photographers" "your state." There are also many general directories, too, like photojournalist sites, theknot.com and my new site called theweddingpicture.biz.

Bridal magazines: Check the local ads in them to find a photographer.

Event planners/caterers: A lot of wedding planners like to work with selected photographers because they know the venues, they work well with these photographers, they know their style and work ethics. They know there won't be any problems so if you're using a wedding planner, take their recommendation seriously. Also, the banquet manager at your venue might have a few suggestions.

CHEMISTRY

Once you've selected a few photographers whose work you love and who fit into your budget, how do you make the final decision? To me, the most important thing in choosing a photographer is chemistry.

Do you think you will feel uncomfortable being undressed in a room with this person when you're getting ready? (This is why some brides prefer female photographers.) Can you call or email this person about the most trivial thing about your wedding and not feel like you're bothering them? Do you feel relaxed with them? If you don't feel relaxed, then how will you be able to feel relaxed with them on your actual wedding day ?

TIP: Once you've made your selection, have them take some engagement pictures of you, whether or not they're included in your package. It's a good way to get to know the photographer. You'll be more comfortable with them on the day of the wedding and you'll get to see how you photograph together so any adjustments can be made.

This is really important because for example, if you blink a lot, then the photographer knows they will have to take extra pictures. If it looks like you have a double chin at some angles, the photographer can take notes and then try not to shoot at those angles during the formal shots at the wedding. But most importantly, you'll have some great pictures and you'll have some to send to your local newspaper or put in a nice frame.

WHO NOT TO HIRE
Do not hire a friend, a cousin or anyone else you know to shoot your wedding. Remember the old saying "Do not mix business with pleasure." It's true even for weddings. Actually, let me rephrase that – it's true *especially* for weddings.

If you insist on having a friend who's hopefully a professional to take pictures for you, do not ask them to do it as a wedding present. The photographer will generally oblige but be incredibly stressed out because they don't want to disappoint you. It will end up costing them too much money. Even if you offer to pay the friend, please resist. If something should go wrong, you will have ruined a friendship. Spend the money. All you have is your memories and your photographs.

You can let them taks some pictures on the side, but invest in another photographer. And make sure the friend doesn't get in the way of the hired photographer! I once was hired to shoot a wedding where the friend spent 15 minutes taking portraits of the bride and groom. When it was finally my turn to take the portraits, the bride and groom were tired of getting their picture taken and were ready to move on to the group shots.

Do not hire someone who is a different kind of photographer and is "just getting into weddings." It's one thing if a fashion photographer moonlights doing weddings they might bring a great perspective to it. But make sure they have enough experience shooting weddings before you hire them. Wedding photography is totally different than fashion or still life photography. Experience is everything.

EXPERIENCE

What if you hired the fashion photographer who wants to start shooting weddings? (Translation: business is slow.) He's shown you that he takes great people pictures. You know that he can make you look beautiful in his pictures. He'd bring a great perspective to your wedding. So hire him, if it's in your budget as an additional shooter. But make sure you also have someone there who's shot a lot of weddings and get all the other shots.

To explain why experience counts, let me quote from a few people their complaints about their wedding photographs:

"There are about 200 pictures of my friend's gorgeous date – the beautiful blonde in the red dress that I could care less about and will never see again."
Experienced photographers notice the relationships of people and make it a point not to overshoot insignificant people.

"Enough of the cute kid – he's in more pictures than me!"
Experienced photographers won't overshoot the wrong people.
They know that the bride, groom, their families and the bridal party
are the most important.

"The photographer missed the toasts - he was eating."
A photographer with a lot of experience knows to check in with the
bride and groom before he takes a break (which is always difficult)
to make sure he won't miss any key moments.

"The photographer missed the last hour of the wedding because
she ran out of film."
Don't even tell me about stuff like this! Same for "I ran out of batteries!"

And this is just a funny story. Although the photographer had
assisted many times, she had never shot her own wedding. To
quote the bride: "Everyone was walking down the aisle. The groom
entered and went to the altar. The photographer turned around and
took a candid of him. I was standing at the entrance and thought
this was great. But he kept clicking. Next thing I knew I've walked
down the aisle with my dad – the one picture I wanted the most-
and I find myself tapping the photographer on the shoulder to let
him know I had arrived. No pictures of me and Dad." It was too
late because the photographer forgot to anticipate the next moment.
So experience is very important.

On the other hand, being a photographer is a tricky business. Most
of us have had many technical problems over the years with our
cameras. But hopefully, our experience and professionalism have
made them so insignificant that you've never even noticed.

When I used to hire other photographers to work with me, I made
sure we went through the following checklist of "Must Have
Shots." I encouraged them to take a few that were formal but then
to try to rethink the shot in an original way. I never wanted to look
at those clichéd wedding pictures and neither should you.

MUST HAVE WEDDING SHOTS

- ❏ Bride getting ready
- ❏ Bride's dress still life
- ❏ Groom getting ready
- ❏ Shot of venue
- ❏ Interesting signage or written things – invitation, band list, toasts written down, name of couple posted at venue, etc.
- ❏ Ceremony close ups of couple
- ❏ Ceremony long shot
- ❏ Ceremony procession
- ❏ Kiss during ceremony
- ❏ Walking down the aisle
- ❏ Details of flowers on tables
- ❏ Room shot of reception with candles lit
- ❏ First dance, bride and groom, parents, bride and dad dancing, etc.
- ❏ Toasts and reactions to toasts
- ❏ Cake shots, cake cutting
- ❏ Fun friend shots- best friends, cousins, etc.
- ❏ Fun details- bride and groom's shoes, rings, etc.

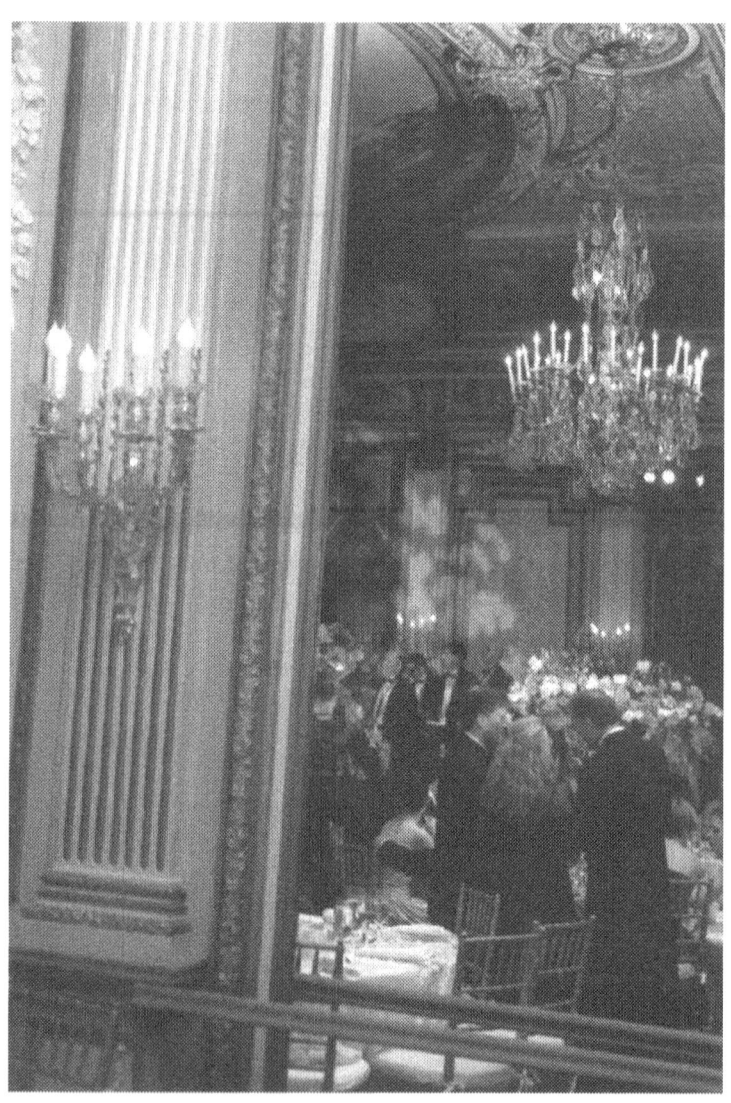

WORKING WITH THE PHOTOGRAPHER AND THE LOCATION

If the photographer has never taken pictures at the location before, ask if you can do a walkthrough together. It's not totally necessary but if it's convenient for both of you, it doesn't hurt to work together and find specific spots you'd like as backdrops.

If the venue has a good website with pictures of the rooms, you can look at that together, too. You also want to make sure that if you take group shots, for example in the dining room, you won't be in the way while the waiters are setting up beforehand. Usually, the site manager has some great suggestions where to take the pictures.

Find out from the site manager if there are any restrictions for photographers- what's the earliest they can come to set up, do they need an insurance certificate, etc. Usually, at one of your meetings with the manager, they'll explain all of this to you.

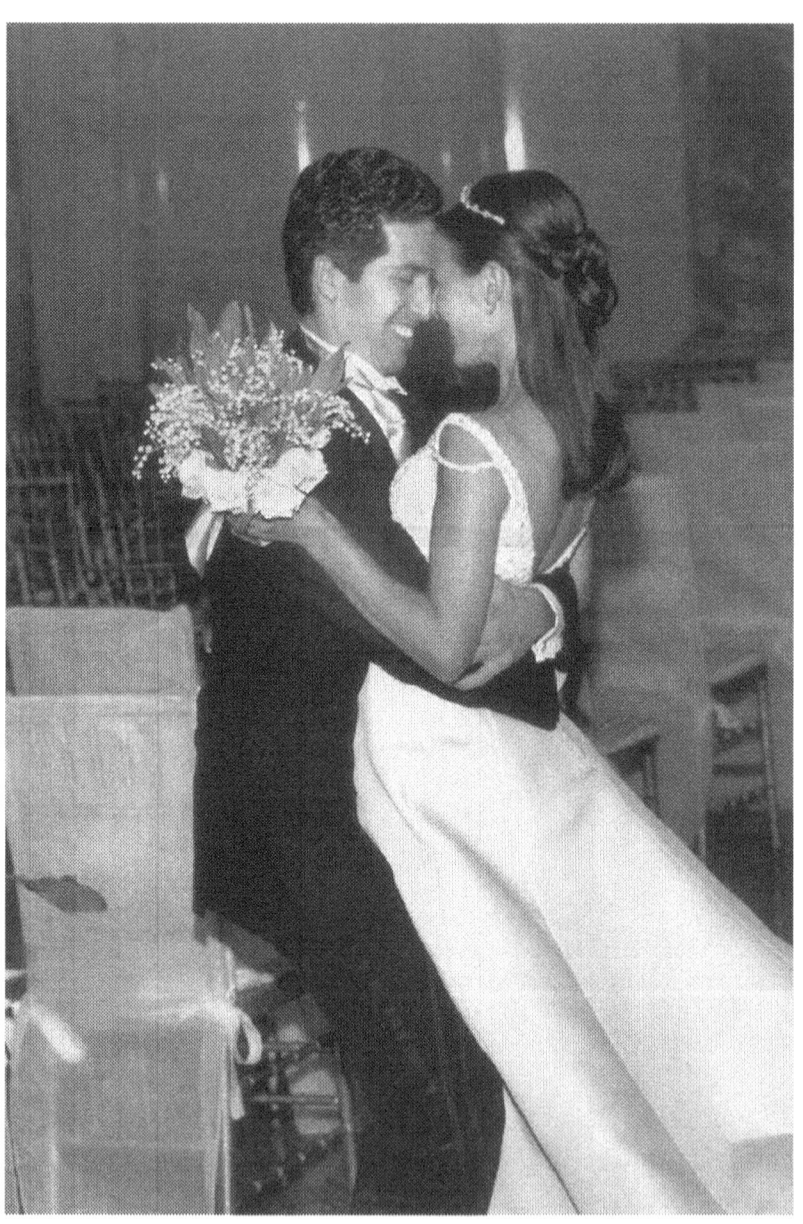

ORGANIZATION OF "MUST HAVE" SHOTS

I've had the opportunity to put together hundreds of albums for brides and grooms. The one thing I've learned is that no matter how many creative pictures the photographer has taken, if there aren't certain people combinations, the bride and groom are going to be unhappy.

Don't assume. We don't know your Aunt Sally. We don't know Lisa is your best friend.

TELL US!! Write it down. Create a list of "Must Have Shots." Designate a "point" person to point them out to the photographer. And make sure that person is assertive and outgoing- not someone shy who isn't good at taking charge.

Most of us who shoot a lot of weddings know what's generically important to document. We know to cover all the "moments." But if there's something else you really want, let the photographer know. Believe me, it makes it much more interesting for us!

Think of taking pictures this way: this is a photo shoot and you're the art director. So if the guy at Table 5 is the guy who fixed you up, by all means, let's photograph him with you. If your dog is all dressed up in a doggie tux for the wedding, well, that should be the opening shot in your album! These are important parts of the story of your wedding so make sure the photographer is aware of them. And again, put it in writing so you don't have to think about re-minding the photographer. It's easier for us to work off a checklist than having to bother you every five seconds.

So remember, it's the people shots that are important. You MUST make a list of these shots. Ideally, you would email it to the photographer at least a week in advance so they can go over it with you. This is one of the most important things you can do so you can actually enjoy your wedding. You shouldn't have to micromanage the photography once you're partying!

At the same time, don't go overboard. Keep it to approximately 10 group shots. And if you intend to shoot your father's whole side of the family with all the cousins, aunts, grandnieces and nephews - about 50 people – in one group shot, make sure you tell the photographer you intend to do this. Make sure that you schedule the time to take that picture in an appropriate way so it doesn't inconvenience all the guests or interrupts the flow of the wedding too much. (You don't want to spontaneously take this picture when the wait staff is bringing out all the food, for example.)

In polling various acquaintances about their wedding pictures taken by other photographers, the most negative comments I've received were:

"There are no pictures of me and my best friend/my cousin Grace."

"I really wanted a picture of my niece and nephew so I could surprise their family for Christmas with a framed enlargement but the photographer never took any of them."

"There are no pictures of my friends- all the casually posed shots are of the groom's friends."

To these comments I always ask - Did you make a list so the photographer knew to take pictures of those setups? And the answer is always no. Remember, the photographer doesn't know who's important in your life so it's important for you to communicate anything you want.

GETTING READY SHOTS

Generally, photographers love taking these pictures. There's all the anticipation and emotion in them. Everyone and everything looks beautiful and fresh.

But here's my big advice. If the hair and make up person says it's going to take an hour, they're lying. It will take two hours. And you know whose time that generally runs into? The photographer's. The person you paid the big bucks to get the nice posed shots before the wedding!

I'd say in about 50 of the weddings I've shot, the bride is running late. In our many phone and email conversations we made up a schedule. In that schedule we allotted 45 minutes for group shots of mom, dad, Aunt Mary and the whole other side of the family from Texas that haven't been together in 4 years. And now, because you're late, we've got 10 minutes to take all those pictures. It's just not fair. We want to do our jobs well. Don't do this to us. Give us our time. It just creates too much stress otherwise. We're stressed, you're stressed. And in the pictures you've got a forced smile because you're trying to hide the fact that this rushing has totally stressed you out. And then you're stuck with the pictures. Your kids are stuck with them. Your grandkids are stuck with them too.

Please show respect for the photographer's time. You're paying them after all to do a great job so don't create obstacles for them! And remind your other vendors to be respectful of the photographer's time, too.

A NOTE ON MAKEUP FOR THE BRIDE

I asked Lynda Eichner, a friend of mine who is one of New York's best celebrity makeup artists if she could give some advice for brides about being makeup and photography. This is what she said:

Keep it classic. You don't want to look back at your pictures ten years from now and say "What was I thinking?" You also want your fiancé to recognize you as you come down the aisle.

Have your hair done first – you want to avoid having your makeup blown dry or spritzed with hair product.

Choose either a strong eye or a strong lip- not both. You are already the center of attention and don't need your makeup to take over.

Choose classic colors that work best with your skin tone- save the fluorescents for another occasion.

Use loose powder to set your makeup, applying it with a velour puff. (You don't want to use one that's abrasive). You can carry a compact powder for touching up. Also remember to bring your lipstick with you for touching up.

Drink plenty of water, exercise and eat healthy- and above all, STAY OUT OF THE SUN!! There is nothing worse than a sun-damaged bride!

And to that I'll add – yes, the tan marks will definitely show up in the pictures so be careful about your tan. And just don't overdo it with the makeup. I've had brides come back to me to make their albums two years after the wedding. They held off because they hated how they looked in the pictures – they hated their glamorous makeup. "It's not me," they'd say. Yes, it did look beautiful on the wedding but somehow in the photographs it just didn't work. Luckily, with photoshop, we can retouch it a bit. And we can also convert color photographs to black and white so the over -the-top makeup isn't as noticeable, but all of that work gets expensive. It's better to do it right the first time.

GROUP SHOTS

I think it's a good idea to have a few posed shots – a maximum of 10 or 12. The reason I say this is that in 20 years from now, you'll be really happy you just have a record of your bridal party, your immediate family, and your grandparents. It's one of those few occasions in life where everyone's together, everyone looks nice and to some people, particularly the older people, these pictures really mean a lot.

They don't have to be stiff pictures either. You can all be sitting on the stoop of a Victorian porch or standing in a group hug. As you get older, you'll value these pictures more and more.

Make a list of who the members are in each side of the immediate family so the photographer can understand the relationships and make sure they get pictures of these people.

If anyone's divorced, deceased, etc., let the photographer know. If someone's not speaking to someone, let the photographer know. They don't want to make your divorced mom and dad who haven't spoken to each other in 12 years take a portrait together holding hands if that's going to make them uncomfortable. Think about it beforehand, discuss it with your family and communicate this information to the photographer. No photographer wants to embarrass themselves or hurt the family by saying something like "We need Dad to stand on the left" only to find out that he passed away a couple of months ago.

TIMING FOR GROUP SHOTS

Every wedding photographer will kiss me for saying this: A lot of brides are very superstitious and don't want to see the groom beforehand. Get over it! If you take all the group shots beforehand, you'll have so much more fun at your wedding.

When you take them during cocktail hour, you miss spending time with your friends. You're distracted. You want to get it over with quickly so you don't relax. You're running late because the ceremony started late and therefore everyone's in a rush and stressed, including the photographer who has to get 20 shots done in 20 minutes.

Now mind you, that's a lot of time to actually shoot. But finding the 20 combinations of people eats up the time. It's not the physical taking of the pictures; it's the locating the brother who went out to have a quick cigarette, it's the time spent getting your grandfather to actually look in the camera and it's the time wasted because your 1-year-old nephew needs to eat right now! These are the types of normal, inevitable things that make the picture taking process take longer. If you do it beforehand, your makeup is fresh and you've got time, that is - if you're not running late because the hair and make up people took an hour longer than you thought.

PLUS, generally it's daylight beforehand. You can go outside or if you're indoors, beautiful daylight can stream into the room. It makes for much better pictures when there is good, natural light in the room.

Don't try to compromise and say you'll take the group shots beforehand of the separate families, and then do them together after the ceremony. It's a real inconvenience to you and everyone else to have people pose twice. And again, that's twice as much time taking pictures when you could be having fun!

TAKING THE GROUP SHOTS

Designate someone from the bride's side and someone from the groom's side to gather the guests for the group shots using your list. This way, the photographer can concentrate on taking pictures instead of searching for people they've never seen before.

The photographer's assistant can work with the designated person to gather the groups. Whilethe photographer is shooting shot A, the assistant can organize gathering the people for shot B. It makes the group shots – the part of the wedding that everyone wants to get done with - over and done with quickly this way.

It's also nice for a guest to act as the "stylist," too. It's great when someone is watching, besides me, to make sure that everyone's tie is on straight, that the people in the back rows can be seen, no one's hair is in their face and that all the other little details that need to be addressed are perfect! The more eyes, the better.

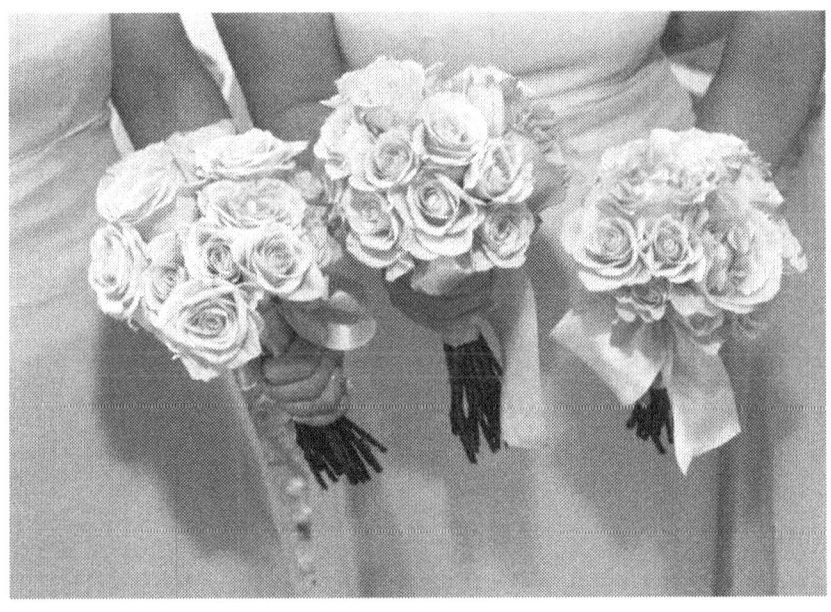

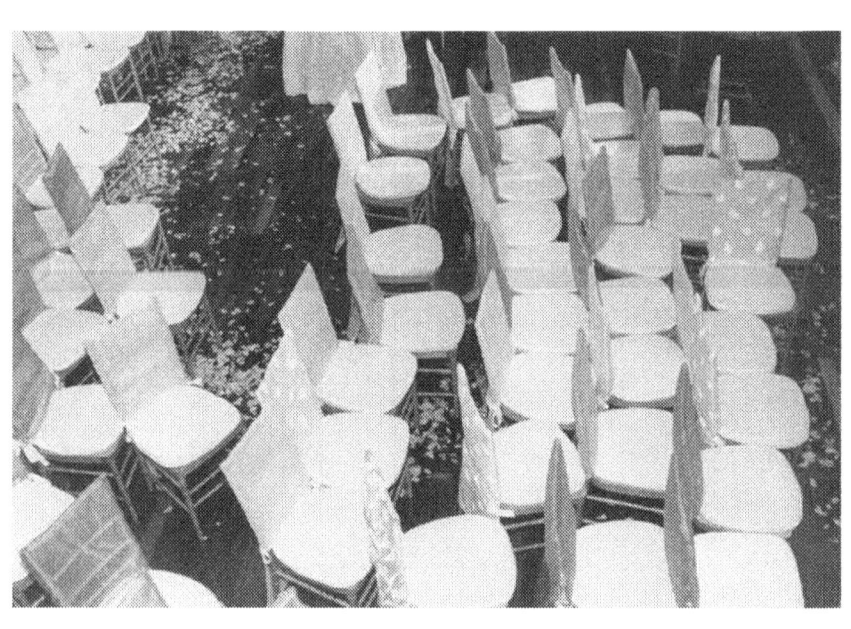

SHOT LIST FOR PHOTOGRAPHER

THE PLAYERS ARE:

BRIDE'S SIDE OF THE FAMILY
MOTHER: _____
FATHER: _____
SIBLINGS: _____
SIBLING'S CHILDREN: _____
GRANDPARENTS: _____

GROOM'S SIDE OF THE FAMILY
MOTHER: _____
FATHER: _____
SIBLINGS: _____
SIBLING'S CHILDREN: _____
_____
GRANDPARENTS: _____
_____

BRIDAL PARTY
BRIDESMAIDS: _____
_____
GROOMSMEN: _____
_____
FLOWERGIRLS/RINGBEARERS: _____
_____

A SAMPLE SHOT LIST

1. BRIDE ALONE – Close and full length view of dress
2. GROOM ALONE
3. BRIDE AND GROOM
4. BRIDE AND GROOM AND BRIDE'S PARENTS
5. BRIDE AND GROOM AND BRIDE'S IMMEDIATE FAMILY

_____

_____

6. BRIDE AND GROOM AND BRIDE'S EXTENDED FAMILY

_____

_____

7. BRIDE AND GROOM AND GROOM'S PARENTS

_____

_____

8. BRIDE AND GROOM AND GROOM'S IMMEDIATE FAMILY

_____

_____

9. BRIDE AND GROOM AND GROOM'S EXTENDED FAMILY

_____

_____

10. BRIDE AND GROOM WITH BRIDAL PARTY

_____

_____

11. BRIDE WITH FEMALE ATTENDANTS

_____

_____

12. GROOM WITH MALE ATTENDANTS

_____

_____

If you have time you can also consider these shots:

BRIDE'S PARENTS AND GROOM'S PARENTS ALONE

_____

_____

BRIDE WITH SIBLINGS

_____

_____

GROOM WITH SIBLINGS

_____

_____

BRIDE AND GROOM WITH BRIDE'S GRANDPARENTS

_____

_____

BRIDE AND GROOM WITH GROOM'S GRANDPARENTS

_____

_____

BRIDE WITH MAID OF HONOR

_____

_____

BRIDE WITH GROOMSMEN

_____

_____

GROOM WITH BEST MAN

_____

_____

GROOM WITH BRIDESMAIDS

_____

_____

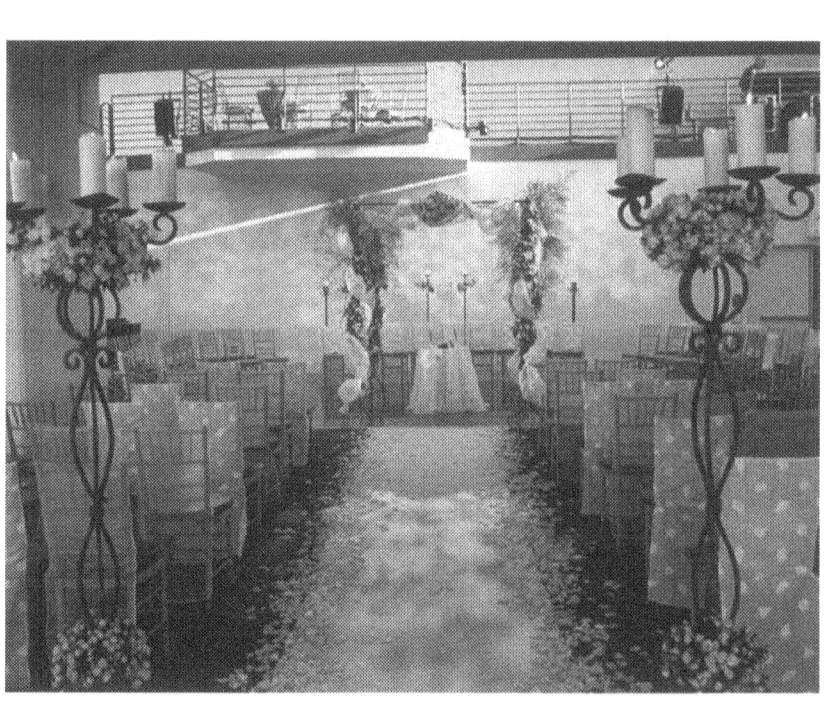

CEREMONY SHOTS

Inquire if the photographer is permitted to shoot at your church, synagogue or house of worship during the ceremony. Also, if it is allowed, ask if they have any specific rules regarding photography.

For example, ask:
Can the photographer use a flash during the ceremony or just during the procession and recession?
How close up can the photographer be during the ceremony?
Even in a restaurant or catering hall, sometimes the person marrying you has rules the photographer needs to know.

And even if there are no rules, think about what you want personally. Do you care if the photographer is standing near you on the altar to get close-ups, even if they are unobtrusive? (Photographers love getting those great emotional close-ups during the ceremony and to capture them, they need to stand in the spot where they can get the best view.) For example, if you're facing the clergyperson the whole time, optimally to get the best photographs, the photographer would want to be at the back of the altar.

So think about what you want and your photographer will respect your wishes. Photographers want to take the best pictures and document everything. At the same time, your wedding is not about the pictures. It's about everything else and your experience of it shouldn't be about taking pictures all day. I've been to weddings where the photographer stops everyone walking down the aisle to get the picture. There are some things, in my opinion, that are better spontaneous.

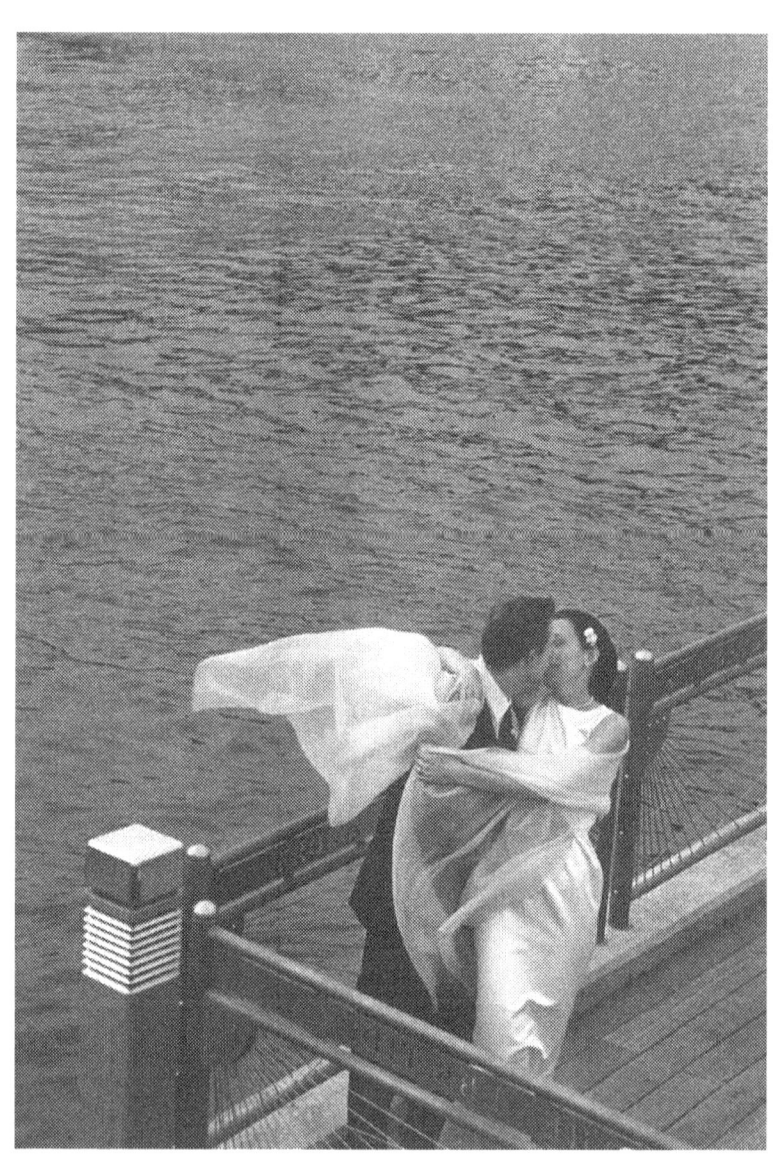

BRIDE AND GROOM SHOTS

Ideally, the photographer would like at least a 15 minute photo session before the ceremony with the bride and groom. I used to like to walk around the venue if possible, and shoot the bride and groom in front of various backdrops.

I always made sure that there are some casually posed pictures of the bride and groom AFTER they're married, too. Why? You're relaxed. You're married! It's nice to whisk the two of you off for a few minutes during a slow time (after the appetizer or perhaps while everyone is getting into their seats after cocktails). Most couples have thanked me for taking them away for a few minutes. It allows them to reflect on everything that's happened for a few minutes and to actually have a semi -private conversation.

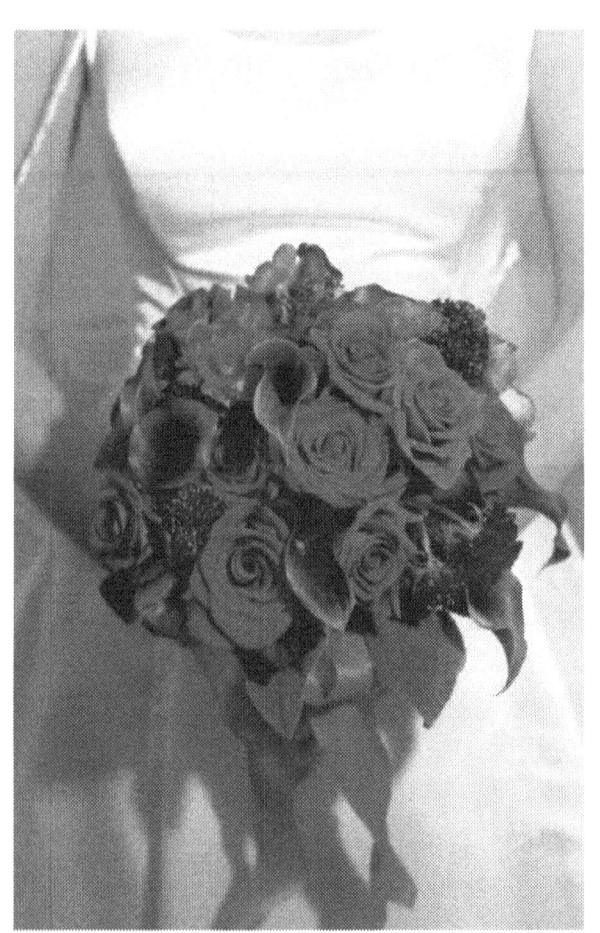

SHOTS DURING THE RECEPTION

A good photographer has common sense and knows to shoot pictures of your siblings and their families, lots of your parents, and tries to balance both sides of the family. But any specific combinations of people you want - I can't say it enough- you really MUST write them down and give the list to the photographer. And then, you have to be realistic and make time to pose for these pictures if you need to be included in those shots too! And keep in mind, that you shouldn't overwhelm the photographer with 50 different situations. They'll miss all the great spontaneous shots then.

Another approach is just to give the photographer a general direction like "All of our friends are really important to us and they are sitting at Tables 3, 4 and 5."

Have a designated person who can help gather the subjects. If you don't have it on a list, don't be mad if the photographer doesn't get the shots. Believe me, you guys should be having fun. If you have to keep posing and thinking about the pictures, you're not having fun. A list is good insurance that you'll get what you want.

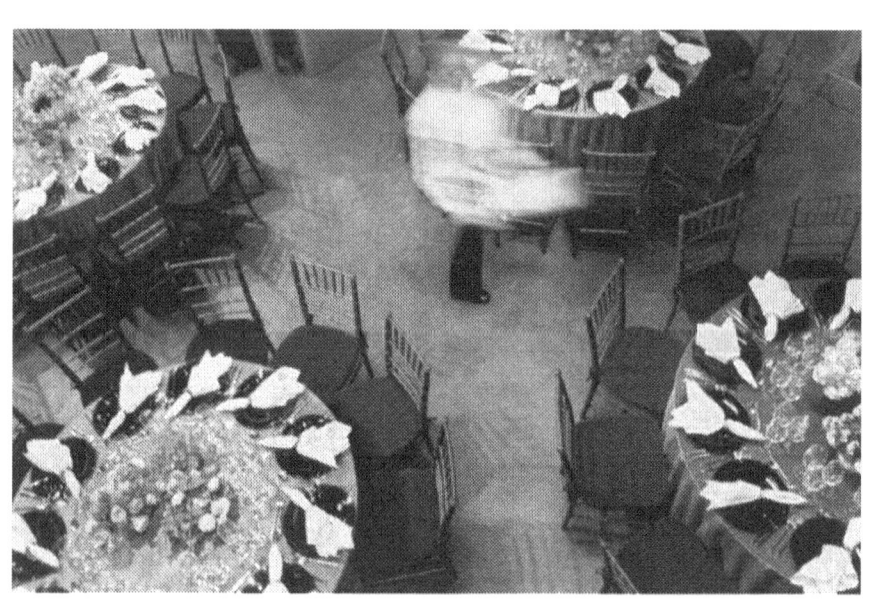

TABLE SHOTS

Personally, I feel that table shots are really boring. They never make it into the final album. There are better ways to document everyone. If you insist, or your mother insists, here is my advice: keep it to three or four important tables- the cousins, the college friends, etc. If you want all of the tables and you have a big wedding, be aware that the photographer will miss taking a lot of pictures of the rest of the party. If that's okay, it's a trade off.

If you want all the action and the table shots, what many photographers do for an additional fee, is bring in a second photographer whose job it is just to take the group shots. But it can get tricky even then for the photographer to get all of the table shots if it's a big wedding. Someone important at the table is always in the restroom or on the dance floor. And when you finally think you might have a chance at the table, the waiters start serving another course. No one wants their meal disturbed by a rude photographer trying to get a table shot!

So prioritize your tables if it's a big wedding and let the photographer know which of the tables are most important. If it's a small wedding of less than 100 people, it shouldn't be a problem for the photographer to get everyone- and hopefully, the photographer will make the shots a little fun and interesting!

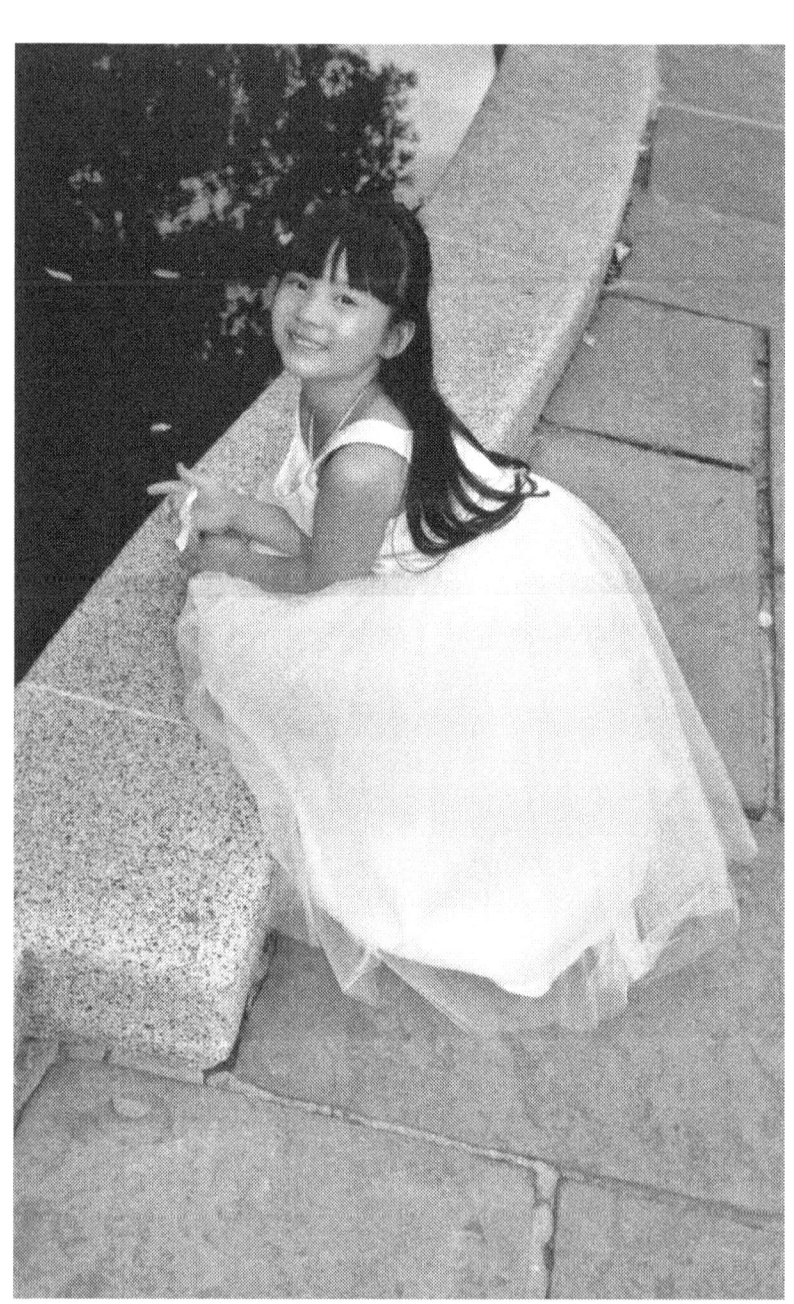

VIDEOGRAPHY

If you want to have your wedding on video, first ask the photographer if there's anyone they recommend. It's helpful to the photographer if they can work with the videographer to make sure they are not interfering with each other. It drives photographers crazy when the videographer is in their shot.

Also, if the video company comes with a big team and lots of lights, it's especially important that everyone can work together and not be in each other's way. When there are two videographers on opposite sides of the dance floor, for example, there will be cross-lighting and then there's nowhere for the photographer to stand and not have their lights ruining the pictures! Photojournalists work best with videographers who shoot in the documentary style – they generally will also try to be unobtrusive.

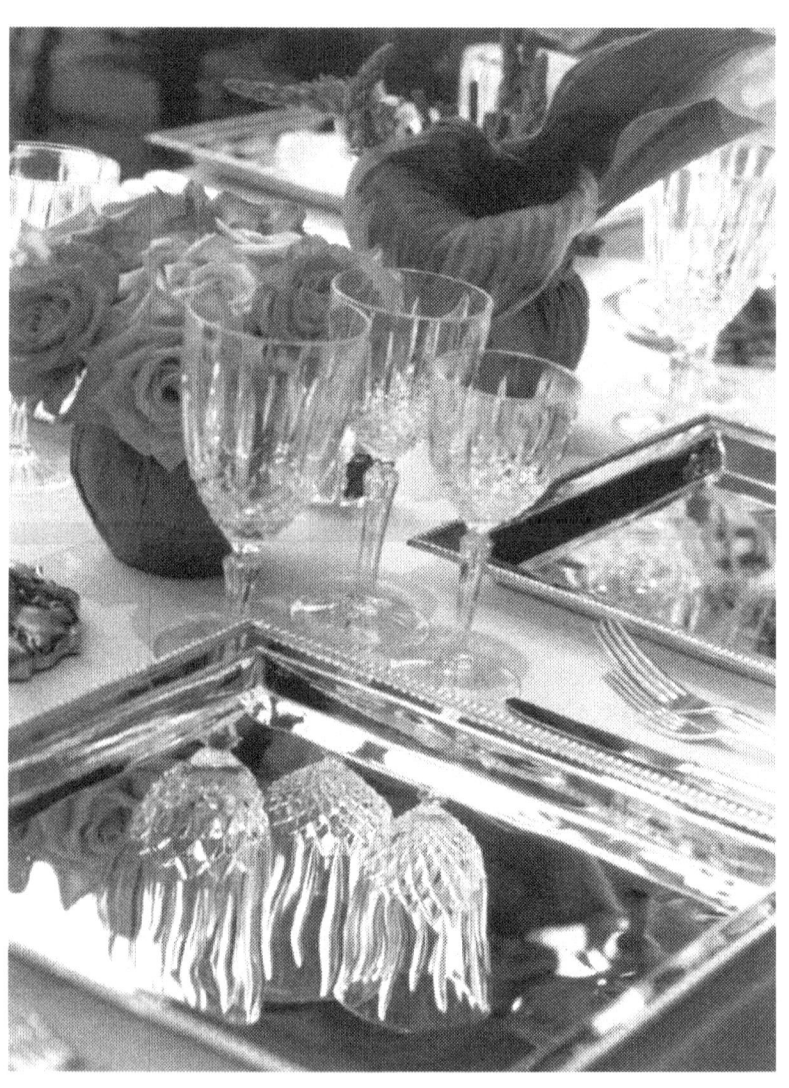

ALBUMS

It amazes me that there are weddings I've photographed 10 years ago and the couples have never come back to make an album. They'd call and call and say they were going to do it. But life gets in the way. They'd move, have kids and then it just never happens.

I tell my clients that your album should be your first anniversary present to each other. That means 6-9 months after the wedding you should get started because it takes time for the photographer to make the prints and have them put or scanned into the albums. It will also get your mother and grandmother off your back!

I think it's important to wait a little because people tend to want to document every single moment in the album if they do it right away. With a little distance, you will select pictures you really like.

The best albums are those that tell a story about the bride and groom. I personally prefer this to ones that have a million group and table shots in them. You can make another little book with those if you want or put them in frames. If you must put those in, keep them to a few. I also love it when people mix in the people shots with shots of the details or as I call them "the Martha Stewart" shots. It's nice to tell the story of the wedding and include an establishing shot of the location as well as mixing in shots of the flowers, your hands, even your shoes if they're interesting!

Some photographers have incentive programs which I think are a great idea. For example, if you make your album 60 days or so after the wedding, you can get a discount on the reprint prices.

My contract stated that the prices for reprints are good for up to 6 months after the wedding. This is because some weddings are booked two years in advance. Lab prices for photographers tend to go up along with everything else, so prices unfortunately have to go up, too.

Do it early and you'll save money. Plus none of your friends will really care about looking at your wedding pictures two years after the event!

STYLE OF ALBUMS

For many years there were only those big leather and artificial leather albums with the gold trim pages that were used for wedding photographs. They are still used by many studios and can be very lovely. But there is a whole world of other styles today that you can find that are classic, stylish and beautiful too. For example, there are beautiful Italian leather albums, hand bound books and digitally created albums. And there are alot of them that are a little less traditional, too.

Some wedding photographers will offer you a range of choices or lead you to stores and websites where you can order albums yourself. Since you've spent a lot of money on your wedding photography, the final presentation should be beautiful. Just make sure you select an album with acid free pages so the pictures won't fade . If you want to put the album together yourself and you've bought the kind of album where you have to mount the photographs on the page, please use acid free backing tape. You can find the tape at most art supply stores. If you're not particularly neat, I'd advise you to have a professional mount the photos. If you make a mistake, it's not easy to correct.

And one more suggestion – feel free to mix sizes of pictures in the album but don't go overboard. You don't want it to look like a scrapbook. Try to keep it classic. What's trendy now might not be something you want to look at in ten years.

REPRINTS

Not all printing is alike. If your photographer is shooting digitally, check the quality of the digital prints, especially the black and
white ones, when you look at their portfolios. Prints from digital
files that are printed at a traditional color lab tend to have a bit
more contrast.

Black and white prints produced at color photo labs (which is the
norm these days) give the black and white images a tint that is not
purely black and white. Most people can't tell the difference, but if
quality black and white printing is important to you, ask about it.
Machine black and white prints are fine for proofs but you might
not like them for your final album. Technology and labs are im-
proving all the time so in the future, this might not be an issue at
all.

If you purchased a web package and are doing the prints yourself
to save money, I would ask around for recommendations first and
then do a test print. If you want to use a local lab, test with them
first, too. Try to find out where the professionals go. Online compa-
nies like Pictage are used by many professional photographers and
they do a good job.

If you're passionate about fine art black and white photographs
for your album, then hire a photographer who shoots film and can
make traditional darkroom prints. If the photographer shoots digitally see if they can make high end black and white giclee prints for
your final album or for those special black and white images you
want to frame and hang up in your home.

THANK YOU CARDS

Alot of my clients have made thank you cards where they use an
image from the wedding on the card. These are really wonderful
and can be formal or fun. Also enclose a shot of the people you're
sending the thank you note to- they'll really appreciate it.

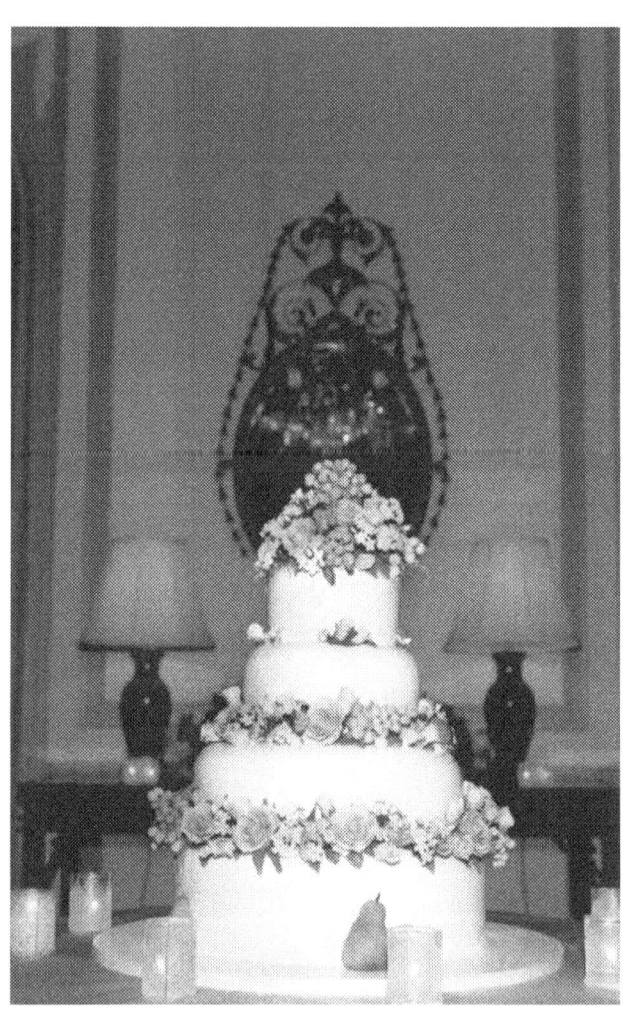

A FEW WORDS ON BEHALF
OF ALL PHOTOGRAPHERS

Here are just a few miscellaneous thoughts on how to get the best wedding photography:

Smile! It's not the time to be shy.

Again, don't be running late. It just makes everyone totally stressed.

When it's time for group shots, work with us. You want to enjoy your wedding, don't waste time by not being organized.

Feed the photographer!! The rule is the fancier the place, the cheaper they get with feeding the help. The photographers are there for 12 hours or more. The band is in a union, they are there for less time, they get a million breaks and a meal. But everyone seems to forget about the photographer! We need a 15 minute break to reenergize with a meal. You're most likely paying for it anyway because it should be written in the photographer's contract. Please tell the caterers to feed us, too. With something edible, too – not stale bologna sandwiches. We don't need to eat caviar and steak, but a hot meal is helpful.

Rethink using throwaway cameras. They get expensive once you've developed all the photos. I've never seen a decent picture from them. Save the $500 you're going to spend on them and use it for a better album, a pricier photographer you really liked, or a second shooter. You won't regret it. What's more fun is if you set up a photo booth or have a Polaroid camera with a scrapbook so everyone can paste their picture in the book and write a little note and make that a little activity at the wedding.

People often make the mistake that when their wedding is casual, they don't want to make a big fuss about the pictures. They hire a "photojournalist" and they tell them to just take candid shots. But after putting albums together, trust me, you want to make sure that in those candids, there are ones with the people you love. So make a list and think about it ahead of time because in the moment you won't remember. Again, those couple of group shots can be very casually posed.

PAYMENT

A little respect goes a long way. Many of you have never been in the position of hiring anyone before. I shouldn't have to say this, but there's nothing worse than at the end of the evening when the photographer has to go up to the client and ask for their money.

It's awkward to us. We know you're busy. Pay us beforehand (as indicated in most photographer's contracts) or give the money to the best man, the event planner or someone else you trust and make sure the photographer gets it before the end of the evening. It's like any other purchase, you go to the store and buy it, and then you pay for it at that time. Some people feel better if the final payment is held back until delivery of the photographs. This is fine, if this is what your photographer arranges with you. Whatever the case, please be polite and pay promptly at the time of each payment. It means everything to us if you are financially responsible.

HONEYMOON PICTURES

And one last word about honeymoon pictures. Many couples buy a brand new camera just for their honeymoon. If you do this, make sure you've really tested it before you go away. It's really important to understand how to use your camera, especially if you want some great honeymoon pictures. And ALWAYS bring extra batteries, chargers, and if you're using a digital camera, extra flash cards.

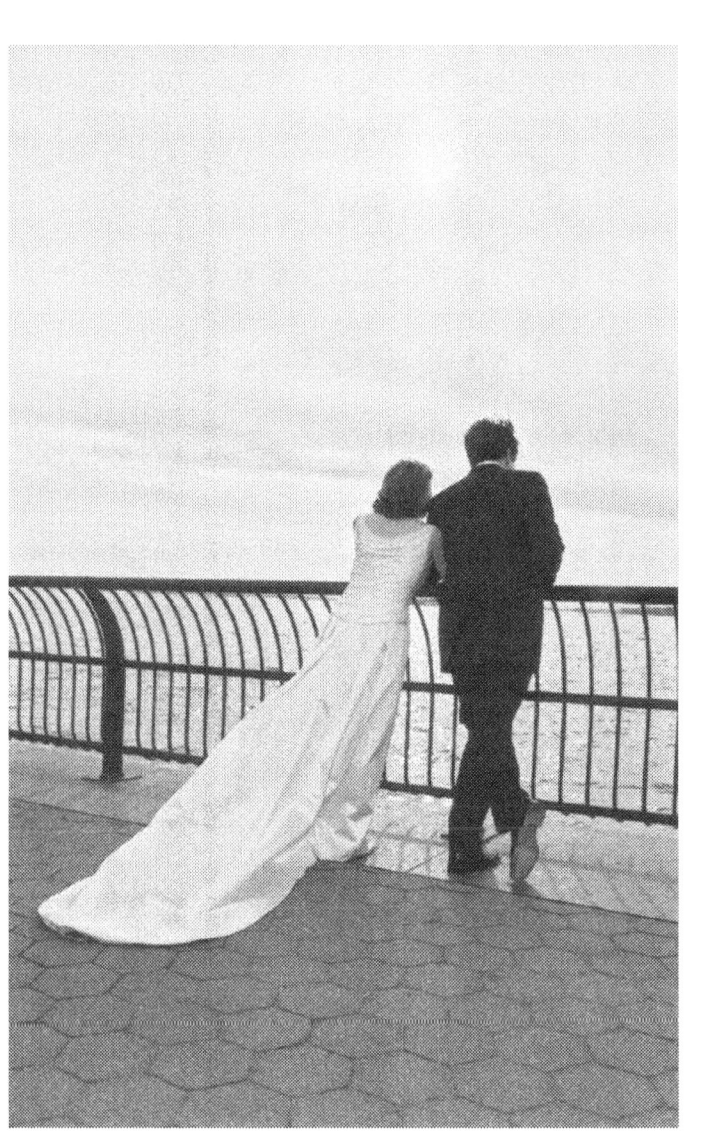

www.ingramcontent.com/pod-product-compliance
Lightning Source LLC
Chambersburg PA
CBHW021927170526
45157CB00005B/2217